John Harbison

GATSBY ETUDES

AMP 8165

First Printing: February 2000

ISBN 978-0-634-01506-9

Associated Music Publishers, Inc.

DISTRIBUTED BY

HAL•LEONARD®
CORPORATION
7777 W. BLUEMOUND RD. P.O. BOX 13819 MILWAUKEE, WI 53213

PROGRAM NOTE

The opera *The Great Gatsby* was commissioned by the Metropolitan Opera to honor the 25th anniversary of James Levine's debut. To assist in its preparation, the Met asked me to suggest a pianist to make a tape, with my participation, of the entire vocal score.

My choice was Judith Gordon. Her splendid account of the piece, in addition to its practical value, was a pianistic *tour de force*.

As a measure of my gratitude I made her a piece, the details of which she had already practiced. The three *Gatsby Etudes* do not follow the operatic chronology, but instead pursue some of its motivic trains of thought. They are pianistically challenging and fun to play. They connect without pause. They are dedicated, in gratitude and friendship, to Judy Gordon.

—JOHN HARBISON

duration: ca. 8 minutes

for Judy Gordon

GATSBY ETUDES

I. Parlors

John Harbison
1999

Allegro commodo ♩ = 96

74

79

84

89

94
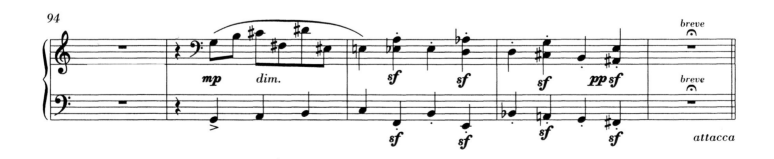

attacca

II. Parties

6

attacca

III. The Green Light

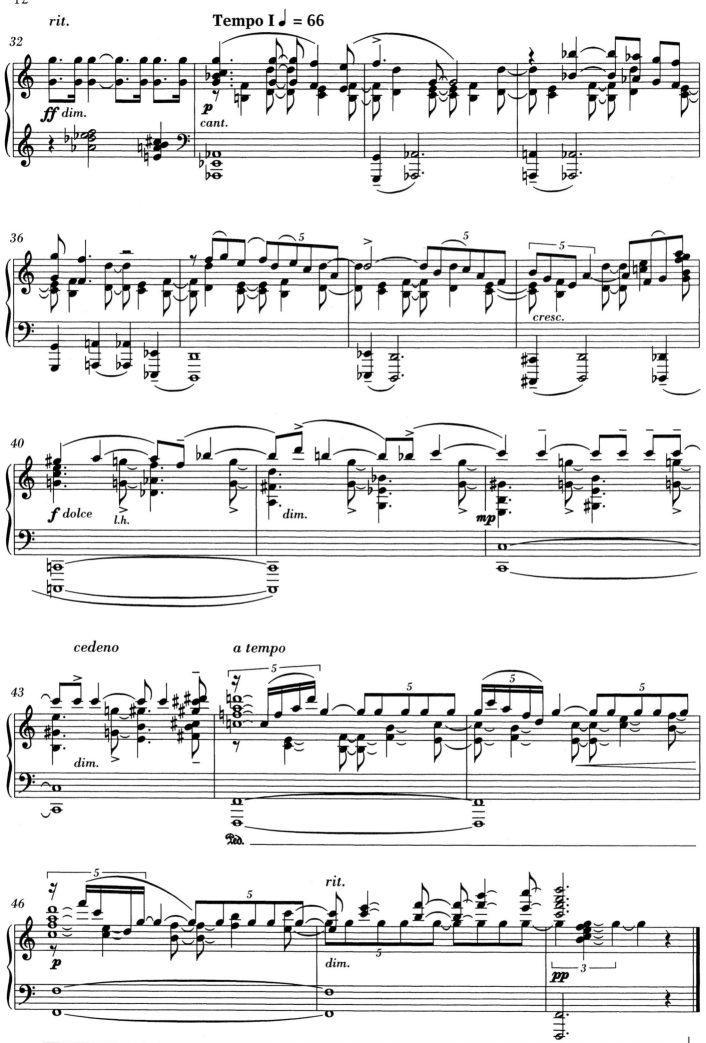